EXPLORING
THE CHARLES RIVER

KATHLEEN ROWE

This book was published by Merrimack Media
Cambridge, Massachusetts

Dedicated to Matthew

INTRODUCTION

We can learn a lot about Boston while exploring the Charles River that flows through the city and into the harbor. As with many population centers that develop along a waterway, the story of Boston is inextricably linked with events along the Charles. The river changed along with the needs of the people. The fishing of the early inhabitants of the region was followed by the commerce of the new Americans, as they established a growing number of homes and businesses along the shore. The waterpower of the river ran the engines of an industrial revolution while providing transportation for a growing commerce. When the people needed respite, they turned to the river for relaxation and recreation.

The river's story has been told in books, poetry, and song and is reflected in the parks and parkways that describe its boundaries and the bridges and buildings that recall the hopes and achievements of those who were here before.

This book focuses mainly on the Charles River Reservation portion of the river, beginning at Boston's harbor and continuing upriver through Cambridge, Watertown, Newton, Weston, Wellesley, Needham, Dedham, and West Roxbury. Travel through urban settings and tree-lined wetland areas along the Charles. Many of the areas described here are accessible by public transportation or a short car ride. Walk along the river, ride a bike, or paddle a canoe or kayak. Whatever your mode of travel, enjoy the journey!

PREFACE

Many years ago while a senior at a small Kansas college, I came to Boston to interview for teaching positions in the Boston area. During that week, I met a high school friend in Park Square for a tour around the Boston Common and a stop at Bailey's for ice cream topped with my first "jimmies" (sprinkles). Then we took the Red Line from Park to Harvard Square. As the subway headed up out of the dark tunnel, I was amazed to see the jewel that was the Charles River basin, sparkling in the sunlight for one brief moment as the train rode over the Longfellow Bridge. I will never forget that April day and my first view of the Charles with the sailboats on the water.

Two years after that visit, I moved to Boston and continued my interest in the Charles, taking bicycle trips from Watertown to Boston, learning to sail at Community Boating, and filming a demonstration of a sailboat rigging for the first video I made on a reel-to-reel video recorder for an assignment at Boston University. I still have somewhere in my attic a painting I had made of the Charles River basin at sunset, and somewhere there may be a slide tape of a river cleanup that my eighth-grade English class produced as we explored a stream in a section of Waltham near the Lyman Estate.

Later, as a teacher in an elementary school across from the red brick Waltham Watch building, I escorted student groups along the Riverwalk to the public library. My son and I paddled a double kayak one Mother's Day at the Newton Charles River kayak and canoe center, and my husband and I watched the Regatta from the shores in Cambridge and the Run of the River in Waltham, biking along the Charles River Reservation from Watertown to Newton—always making new discoveries.

So it was no surprise to my friends when I decided one summer to learn about the river firsthand from beginning to end after reading Max Hall's book *The People's River*. On a beautiful July day, I started in Hopkinton with a camera and notebook, and I have been exploring ever since. I have spent many hours looking at maps and print media then making watercolor paintings and writing about the various sites along the waterway, and every time I needed inspiration, I would go to some area of the river and be refreshed and recharged to go back to one of my projects. My purpose in writing this book is to share with the readers at least some of the ways they can enjoy this urban treasure.

ACKNOWLEDGEMENTS

My parents, whatever our family circumstances, believed in the importance of education and moved our family to a house that was a block away from our school and the public library. My dad had gone to college on the veterans' bill and my mother always maintained her interest in writing. I am thankful for their example and encouragement.

I am grateful for the opportunities I have had to follow my interests and to have my husband Davis's support as he joined me on many of my travels along the Charles River. I would like to thank my sister-in-law Pamela Rowe, who read my manuscript and made suggestions during a very trying time in our family. A special thank you to my friend Mary E. May for her review of my writing and accompanying suggestions.

My appreciation goes to my dear friend Marie Reba who we recently lost and to her family for their support, and I am grateful to friends and fellow travelers Gloria Welter, Donna Fairbanks, and Lorraine Dellelo for accompanying me and taking photos on our hikes along the Charles. Thank you to John and Eileen Flanagan who read the manuscript in an earlier version and gave their positive feedback and to others who have offered their encouragement.

Many thanks to Renata von Tscharner president of the Charles River Conservancy who has provided information, encouraged this project, and endorsed my work. I also appreciated Frank Astephen of the Milford Water Company sharing information with us about the Milford Dam and reservoir and the water treatment process there. Additionally, I was glad to have access and permission to use photos and slides from the Greenway project through Mary Alice van Sickles at Carol R. Johnson Associates Landscape Architecture firm in Boston. I am also grateful for the excellent photos contributed by Jay Pivor and Jenny Hudson with special appreciation for Jay's striking photo of the Cordingly Dam and Fyffe Footbridge that became a major part of this book's cover.

Independent Publishers of New England introduced me to Merrimack Media, Inc., and to Jenny Hudson, who invited me to publish with her company. I am fortunate to have her vision, creativity, and many efforts in this venture, and thanks to Sue Franco for her fine editorial work.

CONTENTS

Story of a River..1

Early History..3

Paul Revere Park...5

The Esplanade..9

Parks and Parkways..19

Watertown History...25

Waltham Historic Sites..31

Newton and Beyond...39

Natick Historic Site..31

Elm Bank Reservation...43

Explore the Upper Charles River...45

Broadmoor Sanctuary...47

River Advocacy...49

Events on the River..51

Visitor Information...57

Hiking...61

Sources...63

Map...67

STORY OF A RIVER

Thousands of years ago, glaciers dredged up clay, sand, and gravel, pushed aside large stones, and carved out hollow spaces in the earth. Then, as the climate began to warm, the melting glaciers formed small ponds and tiny rivulets that swelled with rain and snowmelt and flowed down sloping banks to form rivers and streams. From there the water tumbled into a great volcanic basin before finding its way to the Atlantic Ocean. The water further receded and more land emerged, separating a large waterway into two rivers that would become the Charles and the Merrimack, the former continuing to flow into a large bay.

As the glaciers retreated, Native Americans settled in the forested Northeast region. Speaking the same language, they became part of an Algonquian nation made up of different tribes. One of these was the Massachusetts tribe that settled in a large bay where the fresh water of a Great River mingled with the water of the ocean, creating an estuary that had an abundance of herring, shad, alewife, and Atlantic salmon. The early Americans used small stones to create dams or wove basket-like weirs to slow the water's flow so they could more easily catch the fish with their nets or spears. The Native Americans living upriver from the bay called the Great River Quinobequin because of its tortuous route.

CHARLES RIVER SOURCE

The winding course of the Charles is the result of the rocky terrain of this area and the fact that it is a small river without the power to carve a straighter, deeper channel.

Today the Charles River's official source is Echo Lake in Milford, Massachusetts, at 385 feet above sea level. The Milford Water Company created this reservoir in 1881 to provide water for nearby communities by damming a 108-acre meadow. Using granite from a nearby quarry, they built a small, circular dam between rocky outcroppings at the southern end. Three small streams in Hopkinton, as well as springs from below the reservoir, are believed to contribute to this man-made lake.

Water is piped through an opening in the Milford Dam and passes through a series of filters. Then the river emerges a few feet below the Dilla Street Bridge and begins its journey, briefly disappearing beneath Center Street in Milford before meandering eighty miles through twenty-three towns and cities on its way to the Atlantic Ocean.

Milford Reservoir

Charles River after emerging from the Milford Water treatment area

Charles River Dam in Milford

EARLY HISTORY

Charles River Source

Europeans were sailing along the eastern coast of North America over four hundred years ago, fishing, trapping for furs, and trading with the Indians. In 1614, explorer, soldier, and entrepreneur Captain John Smith of England found his way into the Great Bay that he called "Massachusetts" and named the river that emptied into it after the reigning King Charles I. Captain Smith saw an opportunity, and with his firsthand accounts and personally drawn maps, he sought to entice his countrymen to leave their homes in England and start new lives in what would become America.

A few years after the Mayflower arrived on the shores of the New World in 1621, with settlers in search of religious freedom, Puritan lawyer John Winthrop sailed with another group of like-minded Christians. They settled first in Salem, then Charlestown, in search of an adequate water supply. Reverend William Blackstone, who had left a failed settlement in Weymouth and was living alone on the narrow Shawmut Peninsula across the Charles River from Charlestown, welcomed the newcomers to the peninsula with its abundant water. Winthrop and a thousand members of the group moved to the peninsula in 1630 and named it "Boston" after the town they had left behind in Lincolnshire, England. They also called it "the city upon a hill" because of its promise of religious freedom.

Algonquian fishing in estuary

For the next twenty years, Winthrop ruled as governor of the Massachusetts Bay Colony, as thousands of Europeans moved to the area to start new lives.

Making Land and Building Dams

Across the thickly forested peninsula that became Boston was a high ridge the settlers referred to as Tri-mountain because of its three distinct peaks - Mt. Vernon, Pemberton, and Beacon. The largest of the peaks was named Beacon because of a signal the colonists lighted to alert residents about approaching British ships. As the enterprising Bostonians sought to increase their land, they also extended the docks by building piers for the expanding number of ocean-going vessels. During those years, Boston's harbor became a focus of vibrant mercantile activity, and as the population grew, first around the docks and then farther inland, Boston emerged as a major port in the New World.

In 1643, Bostonians also viewed the tidal waters on the peninsula as an opportunity to build dams for watermills and constructed their first dam at North Cove, near a causeway, a narrow strip of land appearing during low tide that Native Americans had used as a footpath. However, the mill did not turn an adequate profit, and the cove was filled.

Early in the nineteenth century, a large dam was constructed across Back Bay, but it did not provide sufficient power, and because of poor drainage and resulting health problems, enterprising investors looked beyond Boston to obtain gravel for the filling of Back Bay. For twenty years, trains carried landfill nine miles from the town of Needham to Boston. With the filling of Back Bay completed in 1880, engineers drove pilings into the clay and bedrock below to support significant buildings that included Boston landmark Trinity Church, designed by architect Henry Hobson Richardson, and the Boston Public Library in Copley Square, along with rows of elegant Victorian brownstones along Beacon Street and tree-lined Commonwealth Avenue.

The Boston we know today evolved during years of rapid technological commercial growth, as the Americans sailed first their tall-masted sailing ships and then steamships, built bridges, and developed train tracks that traversed Boston.

PAUL REVERE PARK

View of Zakim Bridge from Paul Revere Park

On a quiet, moonlit night in 1775 in Charlestown north of Boston Harbor, members of a group calling themselves the Sons of Liberty looked across the Charles River at the Old North Church tower in Boston and saw two lighted lanterns. This was the signal that warned of the British Regulars' plan to disembark from their ships in Boston Harbor, row to the Charlestown side of the Charles, and march seventeen miles to the farming community of Concord, where they would seize the colonists' stockpile of weapons. Silversmith Paul Revere and other members of a well-organized group rode to warn the townspeople along the way to prepare for the British advance, leading to a revolution and the birth of a new nation.

Today, at the site where lookouts watched for the lantern signal in the steeple of Christ Church in Boston's North End, the old North Church of Longfellow's poem, you can find the oval-shaped, five-acre Paul Revere Park, defined by a walking path and landscaped with native plants and grasses.

From the Paul Revere Park, you will have a close-up view of the majestic, cable-stayed Zakim Bunker Hill Bridge that spans the Charles River between Charlestown and Boston, now a signature part of the Boston skyline. Since its completion in 2002, this elegant bridge stands tall with its 270-foot towers resembling the Bunker Hill monument in Charlestown and its cables reminiscent of the stays on the tall ships that were built in East Boston in the 1700s, using the plentiful white pines of Massachusetts for the masts. Leonard P. Zakim, whose name was given to the completed bridge, was a religious and civil rights leader who "built bridges" between different ethnic, religious, and socioeconomic groups in the Boston area.

The construction of this ten-lane suspension bridge was part of the "Big Dig," the massive Central Artery

Tunnel Project that replaced a large highway overpass that, although intended as an earlier attempt at "urban renewal," had physically divided the city of Boston for several years. Vehicle traffic now flows over the Charles River on the Zakim Bridge and underground through the large Thomas P. O'Neill Jr. Tunnel.

The Paul Revere Park was developed as part of a parks project that includes a mini-park on Nashua Street next to the Science Park elevated rail (Green Line MBTA) and North Point Park in East Cambridge. This parkland is along a section of the Charles that was often referred to as the "Forgotten Half-Mile" between the first Charles River Dam, completed in 1910, and the much larger Gridley Dam and pumps built in 1978, that replaced it a half-mile downriver to protect the city after major storm surges had battered the coast in the mid-twentieth century. The parks were designed to mitigate the environmental impact of the Zakim Bunker Hill Bridge construction.

From the southeast section of Paul Revere Park, you can walk or bicycle on the gently sloping North Bank Bridge over the Charles from Boston to North Point Park, where the 40,000 square foot Lynch Family Skatepark is under construction. This skatepark is intended for use by every manner of athlete on wheels, from skateboarders to those in wheelchairs.

At the opposite end of the Paul Revere Park is the approach to the Gridley Dam, named after George Washington's first Army engineer. Walk or cycle along an elevated crossing over the locks then along Martha Road toward Causeway Street. A couple of blocks beyond Causeway is the Rose Kennedy Greenway, a linear park that extends to South Station and Chinatown.

Access to Paul Revere Park:

From Boston or Charlestown, you can see the entrance from the Charlestown side of the North Washington Street Bridge (also known as the Charlestown Bridge).

From North Point Park in East Cambridge, walk or bicycle across the 700-foot-long North Bank Bridge for pedestrians and cyclists that connects with the northwest corner of Paul Revere Park.
From North Station, walk or bicycle along Causeway Street, make your first left before the North

Washington Street Bridge (also known as the Charlestown Bridge), and cross the Gridley Dam.

Public Transportation:

MBTA North Station on Causeway Street, two blocks from the North Washington Street Bridge (also known as the Charlestown Bridge).

Public Restrooms:

North Station; USS Constitution Museum, managed by National Parks Service (a small donation requested); or the USS Constitution Visitor Center.

http://www.ussconstitutionmuseum.org/visit/plan/

From the North Washington Bridge in Charlestown, follow Constitution Road one-half mile east.

Note:
Look for examples of urban art in the bas relief works on the corner of the Gridley Dam building and the colorful interactive bells on the railing of the elevated walkway.

Pathway along the Charles

The Zakim at sunset

THE ESPLANADE

Boston Basin from the Longfellow Bridge

The Charles River Basin, where a section of the river is contained in a large pond bordered by green landscape and encircled by a walk or esplanade, has long been one of the most memorable sights of Boston and Cambridge. A group of planners had envisioned a basin in Boston as the city's crown jewel, similar to that of the Alster River basin in Hamburg, Germany.

During all the landmaking and development in Boston in the nineteenth century, the Charles River estuary had been enclosed in a pond within the city, but when the tidal waters flowed back to the sea, a stagnant, fetid swamp remained. This led to efforts by planners that included Boston area investment banker and philanthropist James J. Storrow to prevent tidal water from entering this shallow pool with a system of wooden panels. The panels were taken down with the construction of the Charles River dam in 1908, and in the years that followed, the sea walls along the Back Bay portion of the basin were also removed.

While plans were underway for the dam, the firm of Frederick Law Olmsted designed a park along the embankment for the children and working people of Boston's West End. Olmsted was the first landscape architect in America and had previously designed New York's Central Park and Boston's Emerald Necklace. He had been inspired by his walks through urban parks in England, and he and Charles Eliot, whom he mentored, understood the need that people have for fresh air and green, open spaces, especially in an increasingly industrialized world.

Esplanade on a rainy day

View from Community Boating dock

Landscape architect Eliot had contributed to the plans for the dam and created a design for the Charles River Basin in Boston between the Longfellow Bridge and the Harvard Bridge (also called the Massachusetts Avenue Bridge). Another achievement of his at that time was his collaboration with American journalist and urban planner Sylvester Baxter in the formation of the Metropolitan Park Commission (MPC), setting aside 37,000 acres of open land, including the Charles River Reservation, a twenty-mile corridor along the river that extends from Boston and Cambridge to West Roxbury.

Eliot's plans for the Esplanade were continued by landscape architect Arthur Shurcliff, who nearly doubled the parkland adjacent to the river basin with the creation of natural-looking tree-covered riverbanks, islands, and a lagoon. Then after the construction of Storrow Drive in 1950, Shurcliff continued to work toward enhancement of the parkland, replacing land that was lost to the new roadway.

After James Storrow's death, his wife, Helen Osbourne Storrow, donated in his memory one million dollars toward funding the parkland around the basin. A granite memorial to James and Helen Storrow overlooks a small boat dock on the Esplanade near the footbridges over Storrow Drive.

Longfellow Bridge

The Cambridge Bridge, designed by architect Edmund Wheelwright, that connected Boston and Cambridge, was renamed the Longfellow Bridge soon after it opened in 1906. People also refer to it as the "Salt-and-Pepper Bridge" because of the shape of its four large granite bridge towers. On each of

View from the Longfellow Bridge

these towers is the seal of Boston and the prow of a Viking ship in memory of a possible Viking landing in the Boston Bay area, as proposed by Professor Eben Norton Horsford, who also constructed a stone tower in their honor in Waltham, where a small collection of stones in the river were thought to be the remains of one of their dams built over a thousand years ago. His theory has largely been disproved, but a statue of Leif Erickson still stands at the western end of Commonwealth Avenue.

Within a few yards of the bridge is the Community Boating Inc. building, with its motto "Sailing for All" over the entrance. The first public boating program for young people began in the 1930s when philanthropist Joseph Lee, Jr., helped the youth of the West End build their own boats, constructed a dock for them, and taught them how to sail. In 1941, Community Boating was founded near the site of Lee's program, to make sailing accessible for all, and today Boston-area youth can join the CBI's summer program for a modest fee.

Next to CBI is the old boathouse of the Union Boat Club, founded in 1851, the longest-operating rowing club in Boston. Local colleges and universities also have their sailing pavilions along either side of the river.

Beyond the Union Boat Club is the Hatch Memorial Shell, the centerpiece of this part of the Esplanade. Here the people of Boston have enjoyed outdoor concerts for many years, including the annual Fourth of July concert and fireworks, one of Boston's long-standing traditions. A statue of Arthur Fiedler, who conducted the concert for many years, looks out from a landscape of trees, small islands, and a footbridge.

Storrow Drive continues beyond the Massachusetts Avenue Bridge to the Boston University Bridge where it becomes Soldiers Field Road. A continuous seventeen-mile walking path and bike trail follow the river in both Cambridge and Boston from the Museum of Science to the Eliot Bridge, passing the Massachusetts Institute of Technology, Harvard University, and Boston University. Today pedestrian and bicycle overpasses above Storrow Drive connect this open walkway with the Back Bay of Boston.
However, it was a few more years before running would be allowed along this portion of the Charles!

Cardiologist Dr. Paul Dudley White who treated President Eisenhower after his heart attack initiated a campaign for people to exercise their way to better health and publicized this on a tandem bicycle with Mayor Richard J. Daley in one of Chicago's parks.

Today you can walk, run, or ride your bike along a mixed-use path that follows a twenty-mile loop around the river while the basin and parklands are alive with sailboats, rowing crews, and kayaks, affording vistas of a vibrant cityscape.

Museum of Science

The Museum of Science offers world-class exhibits to visitors. Wide picture windows in the museum cafeteria look out over the sparkling Charles River Basin with the Longfellow Bridge as a backdrop. You can also take a Duck Boat into the river and through the streets of Boston.

Southwest of the museum on the Boston side of the river are the open fields designed by Olmsted for recreation, later named in memory of Boston surgeon and Naval Commander Melvin Lederman. Within this park, the Teddy Ebersol Red Sox Fields offer recreation to Boston's youth with baseball diamonds and soccer fields. Teddy, the youngest son of sports announcer Dick Ebersol and actress Susan St. James, was an avid Red Sox fan among his Yankee-loving classmates in Connecticut. The twelve-year-old died in a plane crash in 2004, the year of the first Red Sox World Series victory in eighty-six years. In his honor, the victorious Sox team sailed on the Charles alongside the field.

On the Cambridge side, you can walk, run, or bicycle on a walkway along the Charles River from the Museum of Science area, then along Memorial Drive to the Eliot Bridge, and from there along Greenough Boulevard to the Arsenal Street crossing. On the Boston side of the river, follow Storrow Drive as it becomes Soldiers Field Road and continues to Arsenal Street. Watertown begins at the North Beacon Street Bridge, and the multi-use path continues along the river to Galen Street in Watertown Square.

Access to the Esplanade at Boston Basin:

From the MGH subway station (part of the Red Line) in Boston, cross on a footbridge over the highway to the Esplanade, approaching the Community Boating docks.

From the Kendall Square station in Cambridge (also part of the MBTA Red Line), take the pedestrian lane on the Longfellow Bridge and use the footbridge over the highway.
From the Public Gardens (Arlington Street), take the Fiedler Footbridge, which brings you right to the

area in front of the Hatch Shell.

From Back Bay, take footbridges over Storrow Drive from Fairfield Street and Dartmouth Street.
Public Restrooms:

Between the Longfellow and Harvard Bridges, the Dartmouth Street comfort station is located near the Hatch Shell (closed in winter).

Between the Longfellow Bridge and the Museum of Science, portable toilets are available at the Teddy Ebersol Fields.

Museum of Science restrooms are accessible on the lower floor.

Note: Wait for the Duck Boats by the T-Rex statue in front of the Museum of Science. This is just a few feet away from the site of the old Charles River Dam.

Museum of Science: www.mos.org/

Duck Boats: www.bostonducktours.com/

A Charles River Tour boat

Sailing on the Charles

The Museum of Science

A sunset sail with Community Boating

A gondola ride in the Lagoon

PARKS AND PARKWAYS

Memorial Drive on a Sunday in Spring

Beyond the parklands of Boston's Esplanade and the Harvard Bridge (Massachusetts Avenue), the multi-use pathway along Storrow Drive on the Boston side of the river or Memorial Drive on the Cambridge side crosses the Boston University, River Street, and Western Avenue bridges. From here the path becomes more tree-lined and the grassy area widens to form a small park where the Weeks Footbridge connects the Harvard campus. The next bridge right after the historic Weld boathouse, home of the Harvard Women's Crew on Memorial Drive, is the Anderson Bridge, built in 1913, that replaced two previous bridges. The first one, built in 1662, was the Great Bridge that was also the first to cross the river between Cambridge and Boston.

The firm of Olmsted, Olmsted, and Eliot planned the Memorial Drive parkway, with its stately plane trees along the Charles. During the 1960s, a proposal to widen the parkway that included removal of the trees met with resistance from a group of concerned citizens who succeeded in preventing this development.

A few years later, some of the activists who had lobbied to save the plane trees, with the leadership of Isabella Halsted, Cambridge resident, artist, author, and environmentalist, organized a group called People for Riverbend Park to maintain for public enjoyment the one-mile stretch of riverbank between Western Avenue and the Eliot Bridge. The busy roadway becomes a quiet, no-car zone on Sundays from May to October.

Weeks Footbridge at Riverbend Park

JFK Park

This small park, located at the northwest corner of Memorial Drive and JFK Street across from the Anderson Bridge, includes a memorial fountain, granite posts, benches, and shade trees. Flowers bloom during May, John F. Kennedy's birth month. This a great place to relax or toss a Frisbee.

Head of the Charles Regatta

A sport that developed naturally on the river was rowing. Harvard and Yale met for the first intercollegiate contest on the Charles in 1852. While other colleges established rowing programs along the river, a non-profit community of rowers from all walks of life established the Riverside Boat Club in 1869 in Cambridge.

Then in 1965, the Cambridge Boat Club organized the Head of the Charles Regatta to bring together area schools, colleges, and rowing clubs, following the model of London's Head of the River race on the Thames every March. Every October, the two-day Charles River rowing event draws thousands of participants from around the world who trailer their lean, lightweight shells to the starting point at the Boston University Bridge and row three and a half miles against the clock and each other, finishing at the Eliot Bridge in front of the Cambridge Boat Club. Spectators line the grassy riverbanks from the Western Avenue Bridge to the Eliot Bridge and beyond, enjoying the day in the Charles River parkland.

Christian Herter Park

A pathway along the river from the Anderson Bridge to the end of Memorial Drive continues under the Eliot Bridge and into Christian Herter Park. A kiosk for canoe and kayak rentals is a short distance from the bridge, and beyond that is an arched footbridge that leads to the outdoor Publick Theater and the Mary Caroline Herter Memorial Community Garden.

Wetland plants, including tall grasses, are nature's landscape in Christian Herter Park. Concerned groups are organizing to improve this neglected wetland area along Greenough Boulevard.

Walking, running, cycling, and boating are all ways to navigate this area of the river.

Mount Auburn Cemetery

In less than a mile west of the Gerry's Landing site on Mt. Auburn Street is the entrance to the first garden cemetery in America, modeled after the Pere La Chaise Cemetery in Paris. This beautiful oasis of nature with its historic monuments and a high stone tower overlooking Cambridge and Boston is beautifully landscaped with ponds and rolling hills covered with an amazing variety of trees and shrubs.

Community Rowing

Community Rowing on the Brighton side of the river (Nonantum Road) offers rowing to the public at a state-of-the-art boathouse with panels at each end of the building that open and close like fish gills, cooling the building on hot days and allowing the sculls inside to dry.

Community Rowing

Public transportation:

From Boston, Watertown, and other parts of Cambridge, travel to Harvard Square and walk south two blocks toward the river to the Anderson Bridge.

From Alewife, Watertown, and other parts of Cambridge, MBTA buses travel along Massachusetts Avenue and Mount Auburn Street to Harvard Square. The MBTA (Red Line) subway can also take you to the Square.

Follow Soldiers Field Road or Memorial Drive by car to reach this park area.

Public Restrooms:
Artesani Playground on Soldiers Field Road, near Christian Herter Park has public restrooms. Parking is also available here.

Portable toilets are located in Christian Herter Park.

Mount Auburn Cemetery has public restrooms near the entrance to the Visitors Center on the left as you enter from the street.

Community Rowing has public restrooms.

Head of the Charles: www.hocr.org

Blue Heron Bridge on Greenway

WATERTOWN HISTORY

Blue Heron marker

Today when we see Watertown, it is hard for us to picture the landing place at the head of the Charles River estuary where the fresh water of the river mingled with the tidal waters of the Atlantic. In fact, the place where founder Sir Richard Saltonstall landed is now one of the busiest crossroads in the area, intersected by Mount Auburn Street in Cambridge, Route 2 as it continues onto Storrow Drive, Greenough Boulevard, and the beginning of Memorial Drive!

Imagine in the early 1600s, a group of Native Americans fishing quietly along the banks of the great estuary, when a small group of colonists led by Captain Richard Southcot were exploring the area near a natural crossing for the Natives. Their encampment on a nearby hill was recounted in the diary of group member Roger Clap, who wrote:

"We went up the Charles River, until the river grew narrow and shallow, and there we landed our goods with much labour and toil, the bank being steep; and night coming on, we were informed that there were hard by us 300 Indians. One Englishman who could speak the Indian language (an old planter) went to them and advised them not to come near us in the night; and they harkened to his counsel and came not out. I myself was one of the sentinels that night. In the morning some of the Indians came and stood at a distance off, looking at us, but came not near. But when they had been awhile in view, some of them came and held out a great bass towards us; so we sent a man with a biscuit, and changed the cake for the bass. Afterwards, they supplied us with bass and were very friendly unto us. Had they come upon us sooner, they might have destroyed us! I think we were not above ten in number. But God caused the Indians to help us with fish at very cheap rates. We had not been there many days but we had an order to come away from that place."[1]

In 1630, a month after Roger Clap and his group were directed to leave for Dorchester, Governor Winthrop ordered Sir Richard Saltonstall to be the principal organizer of the new settlement that would later become Watertown. Saltonstall sailed up the river to the head of the estuary and disembarked at Gerry's Landing, an area named for nearby landowner Gerry Elbridge, a signer of the Declaration of Independence and former vice president under Madison.

At the western terminus of Memorial Drive, a stone marker on the path in front of the Cambridge

Sir Richard Saltonstall

Boat Club and a metal sign on Gerry's Landing Road connecting Mount Auburn Street and Greenough Boulevard, claim Saltonstall's arrival. Even today this area is sometimes referred to as "Gerry's Landing."

Upriver where Roger Clap and his group had met with the Native Americans, early Watertown residents used wind power to grind corn and some wheat from Virginia, but when this was not sufficient, they sent their windmill to Boston. In 1634, at a place where a few stones had been placed to slow the water's flow, maybe for catching fish, Thomas Mayhew constructed a dam to power a gristmill, the first of many dams that would change the character of the river.

A bridge later provided passage for people and their animals and for transporting the grain from Mayhew's mill. "A bridge crossed near here as early as A.D. 1641. Here by the mill, bridges were built A.D. 1667 and 1719." These words are engraved on the concrete balustrade of the most recent of the bridges on Galen Street in Watertown Square, a busy crossing today for cars, buses, and intrepid pedestrians.

Watertown and the Charles River also played a role in American history by providing a place where the United States Navy could store munitions during the brief War of 1812, moving them upriver from Charlestown to secure them from British seizure. The United States continued to use the Arsenal complex of buildings for military research and munitions until 1995, when it was sold for civilian use.

Commander's Mansion

Near the Arsenal complex and Talcott Avenue, on a hill overlooking the Charles, is a red brick mansion of the Civil War period with landscaping by Frederick Olmsted. The mansion does not offer tours but is open to functions.

Perkins School for the Blind

The well-known Perkins School for the Blind, established in 1829, has been located for many years on the embankment near the site of the Southcot encampment. Besides providing education for many sight- and hearing-disabled adults and children, including Helen Keller and Anne Sullivan, the school offers a wide range of assistive technologies and services to people around the world who are blind, deaf blind, visually impaired, or have other disabilities.

The Greenway

Watertown Square is a hub of activity, and yet just a few feet away from the Galen Street Bridge over the Charles is the beginning of the Greenway, a six-mile trail bordering the Charles, rich with diverse wildlife and cultural history. The Department of Conservation and Recreation and project director Dan Driscoll committed in 1998 to improving this part of the Charles River Reservation from the Galen Street Bridge in Watertown Square to Commonwealth Avenue in Newton, making it more accessible to the many people that live and work within walking distance of its banks, while improving and protecting the river and bordering wildlife. The project included reclaiming land, reinforcing the riverbanks against erosion, and constructing the walking/bike path with granite markers.

On the Watertown side of the river is a quiet, green area and beyond that a wooden platform that provides an overlook of the Watertown dam, where flocks of birds hover and dive for fish. Across the river on the Newton side of the dam, along California Street, is an information kiosk just a few feet from a fish ladder, where anadromous fish[2] can "bypass" the dam and swim upriver. Fish ladders are made up of a series of regularly spaced wooden boards that slow the water's flow along an incline beside the dam. The fish can ascend through the various "rungs" during spawning in the spring.

Roger Clap and his men

Roger Clap and Native American

Another feature of the Greenway project is a series of stones beside the path with engraved images of an Indian fishing and of fish, trees, plants, birds, and amphibians that inhabit this ecosystem. The trail crosses paved roads on bridges that span Farwell and Newton Streets, where heron "footprints" on the pavement, as well as the blue heron granite marker, indicate the continuation of the route. You can walk, run, and bicycle on this trail. Make note of the heron "footprints" painted on road crossings.

The attractive, 140-foot Blue Heron suspension bridge for pedestrians crosses the river between Waltham and Newton just east of Farwell Street.

This is yet another place of quiet in a busy world.

The first etching you will see at the Watertown entrance to the trail is of an Indian fishing.

Images etched on stones that border the Greenway include fish, such as the largemouth bass, American shad, alewife, and blueback herring.

Birds are the black-crowned night heron, and eastern belted kingfisher.

Other animals are the painted turtle, spotted salamander, green darner, and dragonfly.

Trees include the red maple and northern arrowwood. (Images Courtesy of Carol R. Johnson Associates Inc.)

Access to Historic Sites near Watertown Square:

On Greenough Blvd., cross Arsenal Street at the lights, then turn right onto the North Beacon Street Bridge and bear left along Charles River Road (or the pathway along the river). Alternatively, make a "hard right" onto North Beacon Street or (Route 20) into Watertown Square. You will pass Perkins School for the Blind on your left.

From Cambridge, take the MBTA bus down Mount Auburn Street to the Square, passing by the entrance to the Mount Auburn Cemetery.

From Boston, ride on the MBTA bus at Watertown Square.

Public Restrooms:

The Watertown Public Library on the east side of Main Street next to the fire station and two blocks rom the Square has public restrooms.

[1] *These words are found on a small stone on the riverbank a short distance from Watertown Square (along Charles River Road)*
[2] *Anadromous fish live in both fresh and salt water. They swim upriver from the estuary to fresh water to mate.*

Waltham Watch Factory building

WALTHAM HISTORIC SITES

Moody Street Dam and fish ladder

Francis Cabot Lowell found a business opportunity in a twelve-foot waterfall on the Charles River, the site of a paper mill in the quiet, rural town of Waltham. The early 1800s was a very challenging time for his import shipping company because of conflict between Britain and France that led to embargoes and American sailors being impressed into service by the British Navy, events that would lead to the brief War of 1812. Lowell then took his family on a vacation to England, where he observed and memorized the successful operations of water-powered textile mills. When he returned to America, Lowell and brother-in-law Patrick Tracy sought financial backing from a group of business colleagues and enlisted friend and mechanic Paul Moody to help raise the dam for increased hydropower and to construct a mill similar to what he had seen in Britain. His textile mill would be the first in this country to turn cotton into cloth under one roof.

This entrepreneur of the industrial revolution invited workers who were part of a "cottage industry," producing small amounts of cotton on spinning wheels in their homes, to work at his Boston Manufacturing Company. He built housing for his employees, many of them young women coming from their farms to earn money for their families and to experience independence for the first time. They were the first group of industrial workers in the new country to strike for better wages.

When Lowell died in his thirties, his investors developed the Lowell Mills, with waterpower from the larger Merrimack River. Textile production became a major industry for New England with its many rivers.

The five-story, red brick mill building, now home to the Charles River Museum of Industry, also provides housing at fair market rental prices. The museum includes among its displays the early textile looms, equipment from Waltham's watch factory, and autos that were produced along the Charles River.

The Waltham Watch Company was established in the mid-nineteenth century a short distance from Boston Manufacturing. It was the first place in this country where watches were beautifully crafted using interchangeable precision parts. Like other brick factory buildings of that era, with its towers and high windows that provided natural light for its workers, the watch factory employed thousands of people. A recession in the 1950s closed the factory, and several small companies now use the complex of buildings.

Norumbega Tower

Plans are underway to develop the complex into residential and retail space with riverfront dining, while honoring its Queen Anne and Romanesque Revival architecture.

Mount Feake Cemetery, overlooking the Charles River, is another historic site across from the watch factory complex. Governor Winthrop had traveled upriver to this area around 1630, and the cemetery, founded in 1857, was named after his son-in-law. Those who are interested in history will find the graves of Spanish-American War and World War I veterans, as well as some of Waltham's notable first families.

The damming of the Charles River by the Boston Manufacturing Company in the 1800s created a large millpond (almost six miles long) with the flooding of a two-hundred-acre meadow. Local residents refer to this pond as the "Lakes District" with its small islands and forested coves, a great location for picnicking and canoeing. The small Woerd Avenue boat launch near the watch factory building provides access to this area of the Charles.

The Lakes District, known for its recreational value in the nineteenth century, became more accessible to residents of the Boston area because of a trolley built near the Boston and Albany railroad station. To increase the use of the trolley, Norumbega Park was created in neighboring Auburndale, Newton, in 1897. The park, called "Auburndale-on-the-Charles," had a restaurant, carousel, zoo, penny arcade, electric fountain, and picnic areas.

Imagine the scene here during the early 1900s, when as many as five thousand canoes could be seen on a warm Sunday during the summer, with observers watching from the Weston Bridge (Commonwealth Avenue). At times, a steam-powered white Swan Boat plied the waters with as many as a hundred passengers aboard. Many swing bands and well-known singing groups performed in the park at the Totem Pole Ballroom in the 1940s and 1950s.

A year after Norumbega began operation, the Riverside Park was built near the Boston and Albany railroad station. However, in the 1960s, with increasing auto travel and changing interests, the parks lost attendance and were closed.

Today, the Newton Charles River Canoe and Kayak is located in a boathouse next to the Commonwealth Street Bridge, with a large dock for launching a variety of boats, including double kayaks. The facility provides information and instruction, parking, and restrooms. Across the river from the boathouse is a small area where families with small children often gather to watch the boats and feed the ducks.

If you are interested in exploring something "off the beaten path," you may want to bike to Professor Horsford's Norumbega Tower. Horsford believed that the word "Norumbega" he had seen on early maps was largely of Viking origin, but most linguists attribute it to the Algonquian word for "quiet place between rapids." Follow the road by the same name near Stony Brook on the Waltham-Weston line.

Access to the Museum of Industry in the BMC building:

From Watertown Square, take the Greenway multi-use path to River Street, where you can see the building in front of you.

From points along the MBTA Commuter Rail between North Station and Fitchburg, you can stop on Moody Street in the center of Waltham.

Boat Rentals:

Charles River Canoe & Kayak, Newton/Auburndale

www.paddleboston.com

Public Restrooms: Charles River Canoe & Kayak boathouse

The Charles River flowing under the Echo Bridge at Hemlock Gorge

NEWTON AND BEYOND

The Charles River Reservation includes a number of small parks in Newton and communities to the south and west. Driving will be necessary for most readers of this guide to reach the sites described in this chapter.

Cutler Park Reservation

Cutler Park Reservation comprises some seven hundred acres of marshland along the Charles River, bordered by Needham, Dedham, and West Roxbury. This freshwater marsh on the Charles is open year-round from dawn to dusk and provides fishing on Kendrick Pond, hiking, biking, and opportunities to observe hundreds of species of birds. You can also rent a boat at the Charles River Canoe and Kayak nearby.

Charles River Canoe and Kayak

Nahanton Park at Kendrick & Nahanton Streets in Newton

www.paddleboston.com

Riverdale Park

South of Needham, the meandering Charles makes a 180-degree turn in Dedham. This park is a place of cool relief close to the busy VFW Parkway.

Brook Farm

In West Roxbury, on the site of the former Brook Farm, the hiker can enjoy several acres of fields, woods, and wetlands, with views of the Charles. The farm, a failed experiment in utopian communal living, was founded by the Ripleys, who were part of the Transcendentalist movement of the 1800s, along with Hawthorne, Emerson, and the Alcotts. A sign marks the site location, and the Department of Conservation and Recreation (DCR) provides tours.
Access is recommended from Newton.

Parking is located off Baker Road at the beginning of the hike.

Hemlock Gorge

One of the surprises of this river is Hemlock Gorge in Newton Upper Falls, a twenty-three-acre park in the Charles River Reservation. The centerpiece of this park is Echo Bridge, the second largest masonry arch in the country at the time of its construction.

On Ellis Street in the town of Newton Upper Falls, you can walk through an easement onto the bridge for a sweeping view of the river or climb an abutment on the same side of the Charles and reach a platform at the base of the main arch where you may speak out and listen for the echo. On the north side of Echo Bridge, artists can enjoy one of the most painted scenes in the country, second only to Rockport's Motif #1.

The Newton Upper Falls area is listed in the Register of Historic Places, and the Friends of Hemlock Gorge Reservation work to improve and preserve this special park.

Friends of Hemlock Gorge Reservation: www. hemlockgorge.org

Echo Bridge

Cordingly Dam

One small area of the river that should not be missed is the pedestrian bridge over the Cordingly Dam in Newton Lower Falls. Walk from a parking area beside a bank of stores to the Charles, where a footbridge crosses the river in a peaceful, tree-covered section of the river. Here you can see quite a rush of white water after a rainstorm.

Access:

On Washington Street (Route 16), between Executive Park Road and Grove Street, almost in view of the highway (I-95) is the parking area next to a group of stores, that includes the historic Ware Paper Mill building (1790. You may also park on Washington Street near the bridge that connects Newton Lower Falls and Wellesley.

Note: The bridge on Washington Street has a view of the Finlay Dam and a fish ladder next to a small park along River Street.

The parks described in this chapter are part of the Charles River Reservation serviced by the Department of Conservation and Recreation.

http://www.mass.gov/eea/agencies/dcr/massparks/region-boston/charles-river-reservation. html#maincontent

Natick Historic Site

NATICK HISTORIC SITE

Behind the red brick Victorian-style Bacon Free Library, the Charles River flows over a dam. Years ago, the river here provided abundant fish for Algonquians of the Wampanoag tribe.

During the 1630s, Puritan missionary John Eliot and a group of Nipmuc Indians formed a "Praying Village" on land granted by the Massachusetts General Court as part of an effort to make the Indians conform to English ways. In turn, some of these Indians saw this as a way of achieving security from the encroaching English. So members of the Praying Village acquired citizenship in the Massachusetts colony and formed their own English-style government. They built gristmills with the assistance of local miller Tom Sawin and constructed a bridge downriver, while they continued to live in their wigwams, small, dome-like structures made of poles covered with mats.

In spite of the apparent success of the Indian settlement in Natick, distrust and animosity were seething below the surface between the colonials and Indians in Massachusetts. Massasoit, the Indian who had helped save the Mayflower Pilgrims from starvation during their first winter, was becoming disillusioned by the behavior of the English colonists. He died in 1661, leaving behind his two sons, Wamsutta and Metacom, whom the English had named "Alexander" and "Philip." The two brothers did not share their father's patience and were especially distrustful of English intentions. The mysterious death of Alexander after a meeting with the English led the twenty-three-year-old Philip to suspect that his brother had been poisoned.

Soon after he became the new leader or sachem, Philip began a movement to drive out the settlers, whose activities were threatening the livelihood of the Indians. Although Rhode Island Governor Easton advised him against aggression, believing that the Indians were outnumbered, Philip went on to wage what came to be called "King Philip's War" (1665-7). He worked to bring neighboring tribes into a confederacy, and his men were armed and trained in the use of muskets.

This conflict escalated into the worst war ever fought in New England, with fierce combat, fires, and massacres that devastated the area with great losses on both sides. The bloody King Philip's War took the lives of three thousand Native Americans and six hundred Puritans, while destroying a number of New England towns. In spite of what some have called Philip's "genius," the English prevailed, assisted by the Mohawks.

Philip died in a swamp near Bristol, Rhode Island, at the hands of an Indian renamed John Alderman, who had left his own tribe and joined with colonial forces led by Captain Benjamin Church. Philip's wife and nine-year-old son were sold into slavery and sent to the West Indies. The Indian settlement at Natick ended, and several Indians who survived the conflict were imprisoned at Deer Island off the Massachusetts coast.

One outcome of King Philip's War was to end Native American power in the region, their numbers already depleted in previous years by disease brought by the colonists. Another result was a more independent identity for the colonists, who were not aided by the British in this struggle, thus preparing them for their struggle against England in the next century.

During the Natick settlement, Reverend Eliot, who had become known as the "Apostle of the Indians," had learned the Algonquian language in order to translate the Bible for the "Praying Indians." An edition of the Algonquian Bible is preserved in the Natick Historical Society Museum on the lower level of the library building, along with Indian artifacts, early American maps and clothing, and items from an Indian burial site on the grounds that were uncovered when pipes were laid several years ago on the land.

On the grassy area beside the library are memorials to John Eliot and the Native Americans, and behind the library near the Charles River are two stone gristmill wheels. Across Eliot Street from the library is The Eliot Church, located on the site of Reverend Eliot's meetinghouse and church.

Access to South Natick Historical Site:

From Natick center or Wellesley, drive on Eliot Street to the intersection of Routes 16 and 27. The Bacon Free Library is located at 58 Eliot Street (also Route 16) where Union Street and Pleasant Street intersect at the lights. Limited parking behind the library is available. There is a public restroom in the library.

Bacon Free Library
58 Eliot Street
508-653-6730
http://baconfreelibrary.net/homepage
508-647-6520

The Natick Historical Society offers tours upon request: 508-647-6520.

Bressingham Demonstration Garden at Elm Bank

ELM BANK RESERVATION

Statues of the goddesses in the Massachusetts Horticultural garden at Elm Bank in Wellesley

Bordered on three sides by the Charles River, the Trustees' Elm Bank Reservation comprises almost two hundred acres in Wellesley and Needham and was named for several elm trees that stood along the river for many years. The Department of Conservation and Recreation manages this open land, with its fields, streams, English woods, walking trails, and a canoe launch.

In 2001, the Massachusetts Horticultural Society located its headquarters at Elm Bank in the Charles River Reservation after moving from its Boston location on Tremont Street. Founded in 1829, the Massachusetts Horticultural Society's mission is to develop the public's enjoyment of plants and the environment, providing educational programs for all ages.

Mass Hort has restored and maintains the beautiful Italianate gardens on the grounds of the former Cheney-Baltzell Estate and has established a number of demonstration gardens displaying varieties of daylilies, herbs, and rhododendrons, in collaboration with the Daylily Society, Noanett Garden Club (the New England unit of the Herb Society of America), and the American Rhododendron Society. The organization maintains the Bressingham Garden, created by English garden designer and horticulturist Adrian Bloom, with trees, shrubs, and perennials for all seasons, the James Crockett Memorial Garden, named after the first host of Public Television's Victory Garden, and the playful Weezie's garden for children. Mass Hort also provides a trial garden with a large assortment of plants.

When you go for a visit, you may be greeted by three large, white statues of the Greek goddesses Ceres (goddess of grain), Flora (goddess of flowers), and Pomona (goddess of orchards) that had once graced the horticultural building in Boston and now stand before the neo-Georgian manor house and formal gardens of the Cheney mansion. Notice the interesting faces and the fact that the statues had been sized for their previous positions along the roof of the former horticultural edifice on Tremont Street.

It was the prestigious Olmsted Brothers landscape architectural firm that planned the site, designed new gardens, and enhanced the existing ones.

Weezie's Garden for children at Elm Bank

Access:

The sign is clearly visible on your left if you are heading west on Route 16, two miles from Wellesley Square. The road into the reservation takes you across a lovely nineteenth-century bridge then onto the grounds of the former Cheney-Baltzell Estate.

A canoe launch is accessible by a small bridge on the way out of Elm Bank.

Mass Hort: masshort.org

EXPLORE THE UPPER CHARLES RIVER

View of the Charles River from King Philip's Overlook

Following the Charles upriver from Boston is a journey through historical sites, as well as places of natural beauty. The greater Boston area has many opportunities to walk, run, bicycle, or take to the water. You can also take a longer journey by car to the Charles River Reservation beyond Sherborn and Dover and enjoy the wonderful places maintained by the DCR (Department of Conservation and Recreation) and the Trustees of Reservations.

This chapter offers a brief guide to several places where you can enjoy natural views by walking, hiking, canoeing, and kayaking. The Trustees of Reservations and the Broadmoor Sanctuary websites offer many details, including maps.

Trustees of Reservations

The first of its kind in the nation, the Trustees of Reservations encompasses 37,000 acres of undeveloped land for public enjoyment. The areas described include sections of the Charles River Reservation.

Rocky Narrows in the Sherborn town forest, where the river winds between granite outcroppings, is a wonderful place to take your canoe. Leaving the canoe launch, hike two miles to one of the highest points along the river, which provides an expansive view of the river as it flows through the Medfield Meadow, a Charles River floodplain of fresh water and marshland between Norfolk and Dedham. This view is called King Philip's Overlook.

Shattuck Reservation, part of a network of Trustees properties linked by the Charles River, is also located in the area.

Noon Hill provides a vista of open land made up of the rolling hills of Walpole and Norfolk adjacent to the Charles River Reservation.

Peters Reservation in Dover offers a scenic view of the Charles as it flows through hickory and oak woodlands, its banks lined with red pine.

Chase Woodlands in the Dover-Sherborn area has 2.5 miles of trails. The Charles River Link Trail passes through here.

Charles River Peninsula is located in Needham. "Follow Route 135 east one mile, left onto Fisher Street, two miles to peninsula.

Access: Parking at end of Fisher Street on right (10 cars). Also DCR Redwing Bay canoe and kayak launch.

Trustees of Reservations
http://www.thetrustees.org/places-to-visit/greater-boston/medfield-rhododendrons.html

BROADMOOR SANCTUARY

Boardwalk through wetland area of sanctuary

The Broadmoor Wildlife Sanctuary in Natick is a 625-acre nature preserve bordered by the Charles River Trail Loop. At any time of year, this is a wonderful place for nature study, photography, and hiking along nine miles of well-marked trails through a variety of habitats, from grassy areas to small ponds and marshlands bordered by white pines, cattails, and pond lilies.

Visitors can observe beavers near their dams, wood ducks nesting, and painted turtles sunning themselves. One hundred fifty species of birds include the Great Horned Owl, nuthatches, chickadees, herons, and red-winged blackbirds. Some of the mammals that live there are mink, muskrats, fishers, deer, foxes, beaver, and coyotes. The sounds of spring may be those of wood frogs, cicadas, and peepers.

The nature center building is equipped with solar panels and water-saving devices. The staff offers lectures, programs, publications, exhibits, and group tours, including river excursions. Summer camp programs provide students with opportunities to canoe along different areas of the Charles, explore the rocky seashore, tidal and salt marshes, and learn about native plants and animals.

The Sanctuary is part of the Massachusetts Audubon Society founded in the late nineteenth century that now includes 34,000 acres of conservation land, protecting one hundred fifty species of endangered wildlife.

Massachusetts established the first Audubon Society in the country. The organization's mission is to conserve our resources and research how best to achieve this, to advocate for the environment, and to educate the public.

Broadmoor Sanctuary
280 Eliot Street (Route 16)
Natick, MA
508-655-2296
www.massaudubon.org

RIVER ADVOCACY

The Charles River Watershed Association
190 Park Road
Weston, MA 02493
781-788-0007
www.crwa.org

In the early 1960s, when the Charles River was showing signs of neglect, a group that prominently included members of the League of Women Voters began to advocate for the river, and their actions led to the formation of the Charles River Watershed Association in 1965. The watershed, where water collects below the ground or on the surface before flowing into the river, is important to the health of the river itself. Besides monitoring water quality, CRWA members continue to assist communities along the Charles to improve conditions in the watershed.

In addition to water testing, this group works in many related areas, promoting the control of stormwater runoff and following the demands made by urban development. Early in its advocacy, the association partnered with the Army Corps of Engineers as they approached the problem of flood control in the upper part of the Charles, acquiring several acres of undeveloped land upriver to absorb excess water during heavy rainfall then releasing it during drier conditions.

The CRWA raises public awareness through events, such as the Annual Earth Day Charles River Cleanup and the Annual Run of the Charles River Canoe and Kayak race. This advocacy group also promotes legislation for improvements in water monitoring and works with the EPA.

In 2011, the International River Foundation awarded the prestigious Riverprize for outstanding river management to the Charles River Watershed Association.

Charles River Conservancy

4 Brattle Street
Cambridge, MA 02138
www.charlesriverconservancy.org

Founded in 2000 and directed by Renata von Tscharner, the Charles River Conservancy advocates for the renewal and maintenance of the Charles River Parklands from Boston Harbor to the Watertown Dam to make them more attractive and accessible for all. The CRC projects have included resurfacing Charles River pathways, illuminating four historic bridges, and advocating for bridge repairs. The organization recruits some two thousand volunteers annually to do landscape and restoration work.

As the condition of the river continues to improve, the organization now sponsors an annual Community Swim on a day in early summer. Sunday Parkland Games and other activities organized by CRC provide for active use of the parklands. Other initiatives have included improvement of pathways along the river and their connectivity by adding bridge underpasses for pedestrians and the development of skateboard ramps under the Zakim Bridge in East Cambridge. The CRC has partnered with the MassDOT (Department of Transportation) and frequently with the Massachusetts Department of Conservation and Recreation (DCR), the agency responsible for the Charles River parklands, parkways, and historic bridges.

The Esplanade Association

376 Boylston Street, Suite 503
Boston, MA 02116
http://www.esplanadeassociation.org

The Esplanade Association began in 2001 with the mission of restoration and enhancement of the Charles River Esplanade. Their initiatives include the greening and maintenance of the Esplanade, public programs, and advocacy.

EVENTS ON THE RIVER

Annual Earth Day Charles River Cleanup

Every April, the Charles River Watershed Association heads this one-day collaborative event involving thousands of community leaders and volunteers working together to clean up the banks of the Charles from Milford to Boston.

http://www.crwa.org/cleanup.html

Cambridge River Festival

The Cambridge Arts Festival sponsors this one-day celebration of the arts in early June, attracting thousands to the banks of the Charles River with jazz, folk, Latin, and world music performances, dance, family art-making activities and demonstrations, and over a hundred specialty food purveyors.

www.cambridgema.gov/arts/programs/riverfestival.aspx

Dragon Boat Festival

This Asian-American celebration in honor of China's distinguished poet Qu Yuan features brightly colored dragon boats on the river between the Anderson and Western Avenue bridges. Celebrations include a variety of Chinese arts and crafts, Asian songs, dancing, and folk performances along the riverbank in late May or early June.

http://www.bostondragonboat.org/

Fourth of July Concert on the Esplanade

The Boston Pops have played their world-famous Fourth of July concert for over forty years at the Hatch Shell. Spectacular fireworks over the Charles light up the night sky with musical accompaniment.

http://www.july4th.org/

Free Summer Concert Series

Beginning in May, local radio station 103.0 WODS sponsors free Hatch Shell Concerts, featuring popular music from the 1960s to the 1980s.

http://www.celebrateboston.com/hatch-shell/concerts.htm

The Boston Landmark Orchestra also performs free concerts at the Hatch Memorial Shell, providing classical music, including opera, and playing selections with a river theme while paying tribute to Japan.

http://www.landmarksorchestra.org/

Head of the Charles Regatta

Since 1965, this two-day competition in October draws participants from around the world to race their sculls from the Boston University Bridge to the Eliot Bridge, finishing in front of the Cambridge Boat Club.

www.hocr.org

May Day Celebration

The Newtowne Morris Dancers have been performing in costume for over thirty-five years at the Weeks Footbridge, while hundreds of thousands have joined them at daybreak to welcome May Day.

http://www.newtowne.org/

Revels RiverSing

This evening concert on the banks of the Charles celebrates the arrival of the Equinox with music, poetry, and communal singing. The Charles River Conservancy and the Revels cofounded this event in 2004. It's free to the public.

http://www.revels.org/calendar/riversing/

Run of the Charles

The Charles River Watershed Association sponsors this event every April, bringing in hundreds of kayakers and canoeists who race against the clock individually or in relays, starting at Dedham's Riverdale Park. All levels of experience are welcome to choose among three course lengths—six miles, nine miles, and nineteen miles, with everyone converging at Christian Herter Park in Boston.

http://www.crwa.org

Summer Camping Festival

North Point Park on a Saturday in late July is the site where competing chefs cook using camp equipment and locally grown food. The Charles River Conservancy hosts a scavenger hunt for children while cosponsoring the event with REI, the Department of Conservation and Recreation, and the Museum of Science.

http://www.rei.com/event/42063/session/53879

Sunday Parkland Games

The Charles River Conservancy and the Department of Conservation and Recreation organized the Sunday Parkland Games and "Active Parkland Initiative" (beginning in 2009), offering free activities for all ages downriver of the Anderson Memorial Bridge. Games include bocce, badminton, and lawn toss. This annual summer event takes place every Sunday from June to September.

http://www.charlesriverconservancy.org/ParklandGames.html

Tango by Moonlight
The Tango Society of Boston offers evening Tango on the Weeks Footbridge from May to October. Demonstrations and mini-lessons start each event. Free to the public.

http://www.bostontango.org

Run of the Charles – portaging in Waltham

Charles River Regatta landing

Dr. Paul Dudley White Charles River Bike Path. Department of Conservation and Recreation.

http://www.mass.gov/eea/agencies/dcr/massparks/recreational-activities/biking-paths-and-trails.html

Urban AdvenTours
103 Atlantic Ave.
Boston, MA 02110
617-233-7595
www.urbanadventours.com

Guided bike tours of Boston, bike rentals, repairs, and sales.

Bike Rentals

Hubway Bicycle Share System
http://www.thehubway.com/

Membership in this three-season bike-sharing program can include one-day, three-day, or yearlong passes and provides access to a network of bikes at many locations in Boston, Brookline, Cambridge, and Somerville. Members also have the opportunity to pick up a bike at one location and leave it at another one in the network (first thirty minutes are free). Sign up for a pass at one of the many touch-screen kiosks shown on the map at their website. This city of Boston initiative continues to grow.

Boston by Foot
290 Congress Street, #200
Boston, MA 02110
617-367-2345
http://www.bostonbyfoot.org/

Walking tours of Boston's historic and architectural wonders are available.

Boston Duck Boat Tours

www.bostontours.us

Tour Boston on an amphibious vehicle that can take you from the city streets onto the Charles River.

Boat Rentals

Charles River Canoe and Kayak
2401 Commonwealth Ave.
Newton, MA 02466
617-965-5110
http://paddleboston.com/main.php

Four locations include Kendall Square, Cambridge; Allston/Brighton, Christian Herter Park; Commonwealth Ave., Newton/Auburndale;
Nahanton Park, Newton/Needham line; Waltham location projected for Moody Street.

Artesani Playgrounds with Wading and Spray Pool
1255 Soldiers Field Rd.
Brighton, MA
781-438-1388

Public restrooms are available.

Rowing

Community Rowing (Brighton)
Harry Parker Boathouse
20 Nonantum Road
Brighton, MA 02135
617-779-8267
https://www.communityrowing.org/

Sculling and sweeping programs are available for adults and juniors.

Sailing

Community Boating, Inc.
21 David Mugar Way
Boston, MA 02114
617-523-1038

Sailing, kayaking, and windsurfing programs for adults and juniors.

North Point Park Spray Deck

Across from the Museum of Science, Cambridge, MA.
Open daily May to September, 9:30 a.m. to 7:00 p.m.

Swimming

The Department of Conservation and Recreation maintains a number of swimming and spray pools in the Boston/Cambridge parklands area.

Lee Memorial Wading Pool
280 Charles Street on the Esplanade
(617) 727-1058

Open daily June 23 to September 3, 9:30 a.m. to 7:00 p.m.
Temporarily converted to spray

Veterans Memorial Swimming and Wading Pool
(Magazine Beach)
719 Memorial Drive
617-727-4708, ext. 403

Open daily June 23 to August 26, Open Swim hours: 11:00 a.m. to 7:00 p.m.

Public Transportation

MBTA

www.mbta.com

HIKING

For those who wish to go farther afield, the chapter "Explore the Upper Charles River" is an introduction to areas along the Charles River referred to for many years as "jewels" – quiet, wooded trails and scenic open spaces. All of these areas will eventually be connected by a sixteen-mile long Charles River Link Trail that will pass through six towns, connecting Boston to outlying communities as far away as Medfield.

The Charles River Link Trail will eventually connect with the large C-shaped two-hundred mile Bay Circuit Trail that encircles the greater Boston area from Plum Island in Newburyport to Kingston Bay in Duxbury. The planning of this larger trail is a collaborative effort that includes the Department of Conservation and Recreation, and the Appalachian Mountain Club, along with many other smaller organizations and towns and cities along the way.

Explore the Upper Charles River Reservation

A few years ago we enjoyed some of the trails in the Trustees of Reservations land outside of Boston, day hikes only a short distance away by car. Their website provides excellent down-loadable maps that are clear and easy to follow with symbols for the different activities that would be available to a variety of users. Take a picnic to any of these areas, and enjoy the quiet beauty!

We found the Charles River Peninsula an easy walk-around and very accessible because of the reservation being in Needham on one of the major roads.

When we visited the Peters Reservation, south of Natick, we were close to the road and close to parking across Farm Street, and yet we had a beautiful wooded trail to follow for a short hike that was not too challenging.

We especially enjoyed the moderate hikes up to the Noon Hill ledges in the Shattuck Reservation for its sweeping view of Norfolk, Walpole, and the Great Blue Hill. Then on another day we took the trail up to the King Philip Overlook (there is also a Rocky Narrows Overlook).

SOURCES

Astephen, Francis (Frank). Milford Water Company, 66 Dilla Street, Milford, MA
www.milfordwater.com

Berg, Shary Page. Cultural Landscape Report. The Esplanade Association.
www.esplanadeassociation.org/wp-content/uploads/2012/05.

Bofanti, Leo. *Biographies and Legends of the New England Indians*. (Vol. I-V) Salem, MA: Old Saltbox, 1972.

Carol R. Johnson Associates, Inc., Landscape Architects. Boston, Massachusetts
http://www.crja.com.

Cellucci, The Honorable Paul A., Governor; Metropolitan District Commission: David B. Balfour, Jr., Commissioner; Associate Commissioners: Robert H. Carr, Jr., Avril T. Elkort, Darryl S. Settles, Charles F. Wu, Julia O'Brien, Director of Planning; Daniel Driscoll, Project Manager. *Upper Charles River Reservation*. Commonwealth of Massachusetts (Report) Oct. 1998.

Charles River Conservancy. "Volunteer Stewardship Program."
http://www.thecharles.org.

Charles River Museum of Industry and Innovation. www.crmi.org.

"Clean and Clear." Boston Globe: October 11, 2011.

Cox, John W. *Waltham's Industrial Heritage*. Wayland, Ma: L. Michael Kaye (printed by Students at Waltham Vocational High School), 1981.

Crosby, Irving B., *Boston Through the Ages. The Geologic Story of Greater Boston*. Boston: Marshall Jones Co., 1928.

CRWA. *The Streamer*. 1998, 2002, Fall 2007, 2003, 2008.

DeMarco, Peter. "Bike to the Future." Boston.com. July 8, 2012.

The Esplanade Association.
http://www.esplanadeassociation.org/getinvolved/projects_teddyebersol.html.

Francis, Mike, Superintendent. Charles River Valley Management Unit, The Trustees of Reservation www.thetrustees.org/places-to-visit.

"Friends of Hemlock Gorge." www.hemlockgorge.org. 2012.

Haglund, Karl. *Inventing the Charles River*. Cambridge, MA: The MIT Press. Published in cooperation with the Charles River Conservancy, 2003.

Hall, Max. *The Charles. The People's River*. Boston, MA: David R. Godine, 1986.
Head of the Charles Regatta. http://www.hocr.org.

Hirschi, Rib. *Save Our Wetlands*. New York: Delacorte Press, 1994.
History of Watertown. http://www.ci.watertown.ma.us, Town of Watertown, 2012.

Jackson, Derrick. "Industrial Revolution." *World Book Encyclopedia*. Vol. I, pp. 246-9.

Kindig, Thomas. *Elbridge Gerry*. Independence Hall Assoc.
http://www.ushistory.org/declaration/signers/gerry.htm.

Krieger, Alex, and David Cobb, ed., with Amy Turner. *Mapping Boston*. Cambridge, MA: the MIT Press (pamphlet).

Leif Erickson. http://www.celebrateboston.com/strange/leif-erikson-statue.htm.

Marchione, William P. *The Charles: A River Transformed*. Dover, N.H.: Arcadia Publishing, 1998.

Massachusetts Audubon Society. Broadmoor Wildlife Sanctuary, 2003-2011. http://www.massaudubon.org/Nature_Connection/Sanctuaries/Broadmoor.

Massachusetts Horticultural Society. MHS Horticulture Center at Elm Bank: Buildings and Gardens, 2008. Friends of Hemlock Gorge. www.hemlockgorge.org., 2012.

Massachusetts Horticultural Society. MHS Gardens.
http://www.masshort.org/. (accessed March-April, 2009).

McAdow, Ron. *The Charles River, Exploring Nature and History on Foot and by Canoe*. Marlborough, MA: Bliss Publishing Company, Inc., 1992.

Miller, Sara Cedar. *Central Park, An American Masterpiece.* New York: Harry N. Abrams, Inc.

Morgan, Keith N. Charles Eliot, *Landscape Architect: An Introduction to His Life and Work*, Arnoldia. University of Massachusetts Press, 1999.

Neugebauer, Karl. "Watertown Historic Family Strolling Tour." Historical Society of Watertown: Pamela B. Hubley, Joyce Kelly, Marilynne K. Roach and Karl Neugebauer, designed and printed, 2009.

Newton Conservators. "Origins of the Eliot Church of South Natick." History of the Eliot Church. " http://www.newtonconservators.org/1norumbega.htm.

Pazzanese, Christina. *Going with the Flow,* Boston Globe, Sept. 26, 2004.

Perkins School for the Blind. http://www.perkins.org.

Pollock, Robert. Norumbega Park. Defunctparks.com, 1999. www.defunctparks.com/parks/MA/norumbega/norumbegapark.htm.

Refreshing Tired Souls, Winter Report. Environment Massachusetts. 2006-7. p. 5.

Trustees of Reservation. "Riverside Boat Club - Guide and Trail Map." www.thetrustees.org.

"Smith, John." New World Book Encyclopedia. 1993, Vol. 17, p. 517.

Snow, Mari Anne, du Moulin, Gary C., and Charles Zechel. "Sailing for All: Joe Lee and America's Public Community Sailing Program." *Sea History.* Spring 2010, p. 20.

Teddy Ebersol Red Sox Fields. http://www.mass.gov/eea/agencies/dcr/massparks/region-boston/teddy-ebersols-red-sox-fields.html.

Tougias, Mike. *Exploring the Hidden Charles*. Boston, MA: The Appalachian Mountain Club Books, 1997.

Tougias, Mike. *The Hidden Charles*. Emmaus, PA: Rodale Press, 1991.

The Trustees of Reservations. Find Your Place. http://www.thetrustees.org/about-us/history/2012.

Welcome to the Watch Factory. http://www.walthamwatchfactory.com/ Berkeley Investments.

Whitehall, Walter Muir and Lawrence W. Kennedy. *Boston: A Topographical History,* The President and Fellows of Harvard College, 2000.

Wickham, Rebecca Scibek. Charles River Watershed Association. www.charlesriver.org.

CHARLES RIVER MAP

Charlestown

Paul Revere Park

Cambridge

Watertown

Waltham

Esplanade

Riverbend Park

Weston

Newton

Newton Lower Falls

Hemlock Gorge

Wellesley

Needham

Elm Bank

Natkck

Dedham

Natick Dam

Dover

Sherborn

Medfield

Hoplinton

Millis

Milford Dam

Medway

Norfolk

Milford

Franklin

Hopedate

Bellingham

NOTES

NOTES

ABOUT THE COVER

The scenic photo of the falling water on the cover of this book is at an important juncture in both time and space in Newton Lower Falls where the Mary Hunnewell Fyffe Footbridge crosses over the Cordingly Dam, connecting Newton and Wellesley, part of a link in the Charles River Link Trail.

These falls like so many in New England were used to power mills in the seventeenth and eighteenth century until they were closed to make way for new methods of manufacturing and the leap into the twentieth century with its highway- building and high-speed travel. Close to this scenic location is the overpass of the major I-95/Rte. 128 highway for cars.

The trail that crosses here under the highway overpass is one of many that are now being constructed in the new century, a time of searching for quiet places of natural beauty.

CPSIA information can be obtained at www.ICGtesting.com
Printed in the USA
BVOW10s1525200215

388556BV00003BA/3/P